HERITAGE INTERMEDIATE SCHOOL
MEDIA CENTER

THE HINK PINK BOOK
or
What Do You Call a Magician's Extra Bunny?

YORK ELEMENTARY SCHOOL
MEDIA CENTER

THE HINK PINK BOOK

or
What Do You Call a Magician's Extra Bunny?

Riddles by
MARILYN BURNS

Pictures by
MARTHA WESTON

Thanks to Paul Gutierrez, the hink pink whiz, for his help.

Little, Brown and Company
BOSTON   TORONTO

793.7
Bur

TEXT COPYRIGHT © 1981 BY MARILYN BURNS

ILLUSTRATIONS COPYRIGHT © 1981 BY MARTHA WESTON

ALL RIGHTS RESERVED. NO PART OF THIS BOOK MAY BE REPRODUCED IN ANY FORM OR BY ANY ELECTRONIC OR MECHANICAL MEANS INCLUDING INFORMATION STORAGE AND RETRIEVAL SYSTEMS WITHOUT PERMISSION IN WRITING FROM THE PUBLISHER, EXCEPT BY A REVIEWER WHO MAY QUOTE BRIEF PASSAGES IN A REVIEW.

FIRST EDITION

Library of Congress Cataloging in Publication Data

Burns, Marilyn.
  The hink pink book, or, What do you call a magician's extra bunny?

  Summary: A collection of "hink pink" riddles, whose answers always have two words that rhyme.
  1. Riddles, Juvenile. [1. Riddles] I. Weston, Martha, ill. II. Title.
PN6371.5.B87   818'.5402   81-13638
ISBN 0-316-11744-7   AACR2

WOR

*Published simultaneously in Canada
by Little, Brown & Company (Canada) Limited*

PRINTED IN THE UNITED STATES OF AMERICA

Introduction

This is a **riddle book**, a very special kind of riddle book. The riddles aren't your ordinary day-to-day riddles. Only **hink pinks** are included in this riddle collection.

Hink pinks work like this. The riddle is asked just as any riddle is. It's the answer that has the unusual twist. All **answers** to hink pinks have **two words** in them (like hink pink) and the two words **rhyme** (like hink pink).

Here's a **sample** to start you off: What do you call a really unhappy father? The answer is **sad dad**— two words that rhyme. Get it?

That's not the whole story, however. Sometimes a hink pink has an answer in which each word has **two syllables**. Technically, that kind of riddle is called a **hinky pinky**. But we're not too fussy, and have included them also. **For example**: What do you get if you put a measuring stick in the freezer? **Cooler ruler** is the answer— two rhyming words, each with two syllables.

We've even included **hinkety pinketys**. Here's a **sample**: What's an ice-cream-flavored ape? The answer to that one is a pair of **three-syllable** words—**vanilla gorilla**.

A warning: Riddles can be a **mixture,** and we've snuck some of these in from time to time. Here's a **hinky pinkety,** for example: What's a little yellow bird that badly needs to see a barber? The **answer** is **hairy canary.** See why it's a hinky pinkety? And of course, there's an occasional **hink pink rink dink**.

These are all the rules you need to tackle what's in this book. Whenever you're ready for some rhyme time, get started. In among the riddles, you'll also find a few extra surprises — puzzles, activities, tidbits of information, stories. That's just in case you need a break while searching for a fillable syllable.

Watch out for brain strain!

CONTENTS

Fishy Hink Pinks	8
Money Riddles	9
Bear Riddles	10
In the Kitchen	11
Riddles on the Wing	12
School Subjects	14
Animal Riddles	16
Sporty Hink Pinks	18
Riddles to Cackle At	19
Invitation to a Halloween Hink Pink Dinner	20
Clues for the Halloween Hink Pink Dinner	22
Wordless Hink Pinks	23
Riddles up at Bat	24
Busy Bee Riddles	26
Monster Madness	27
Turkey Time	28
Astrological Riddles	29
Catty Riddles	30
In the Dentist's Chair	32
From the Orchestra Pit	33
Number Riddles	34
Riddles about Rabbits	36
On the Trail	37
Around the House	38
A Hink Pink Mystery	40
Clues for the Hink Pink Mystery	42
Riddles on a Diet	43
At the Beach	44
A Hink Pink Mishmash	46

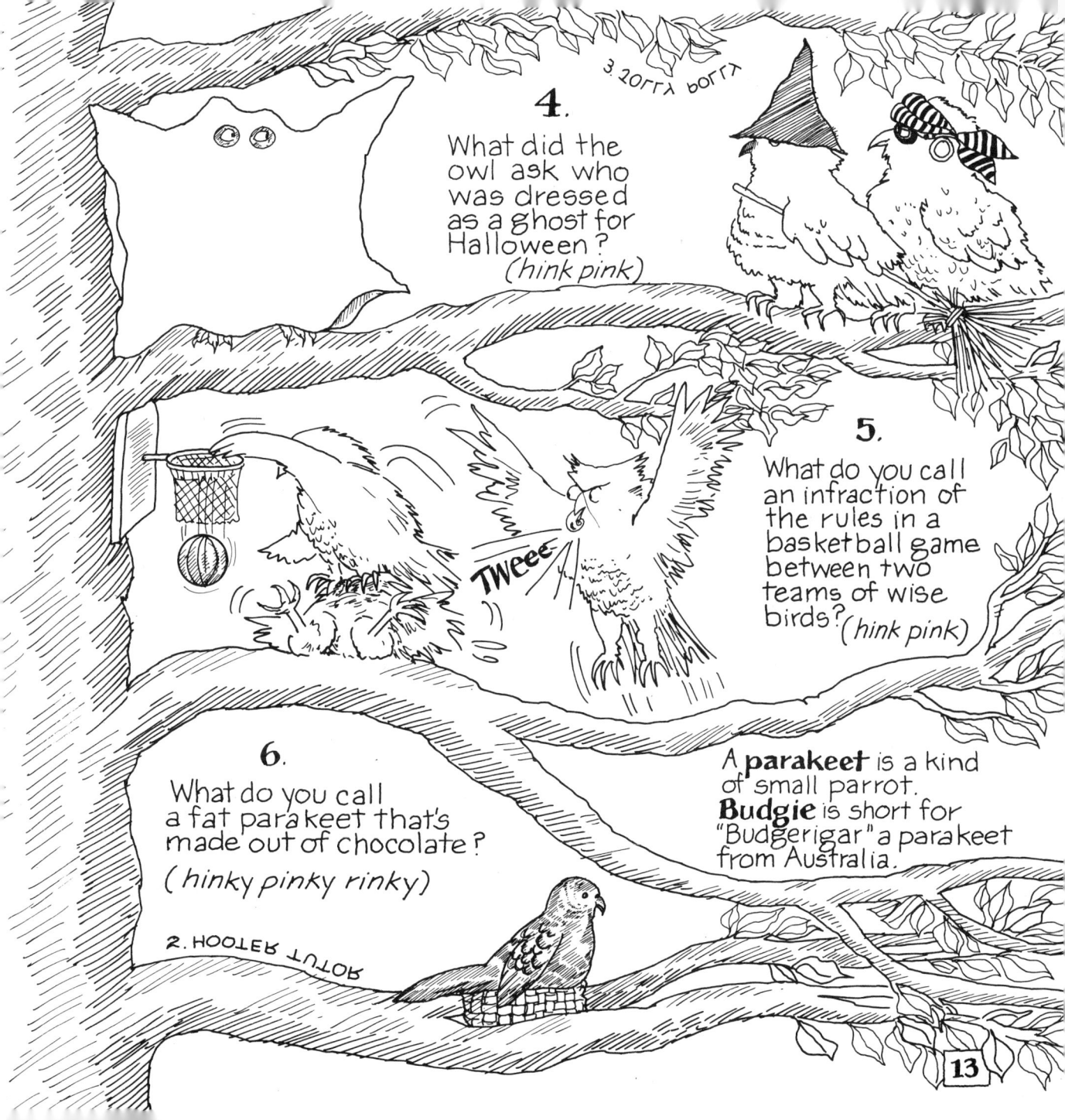

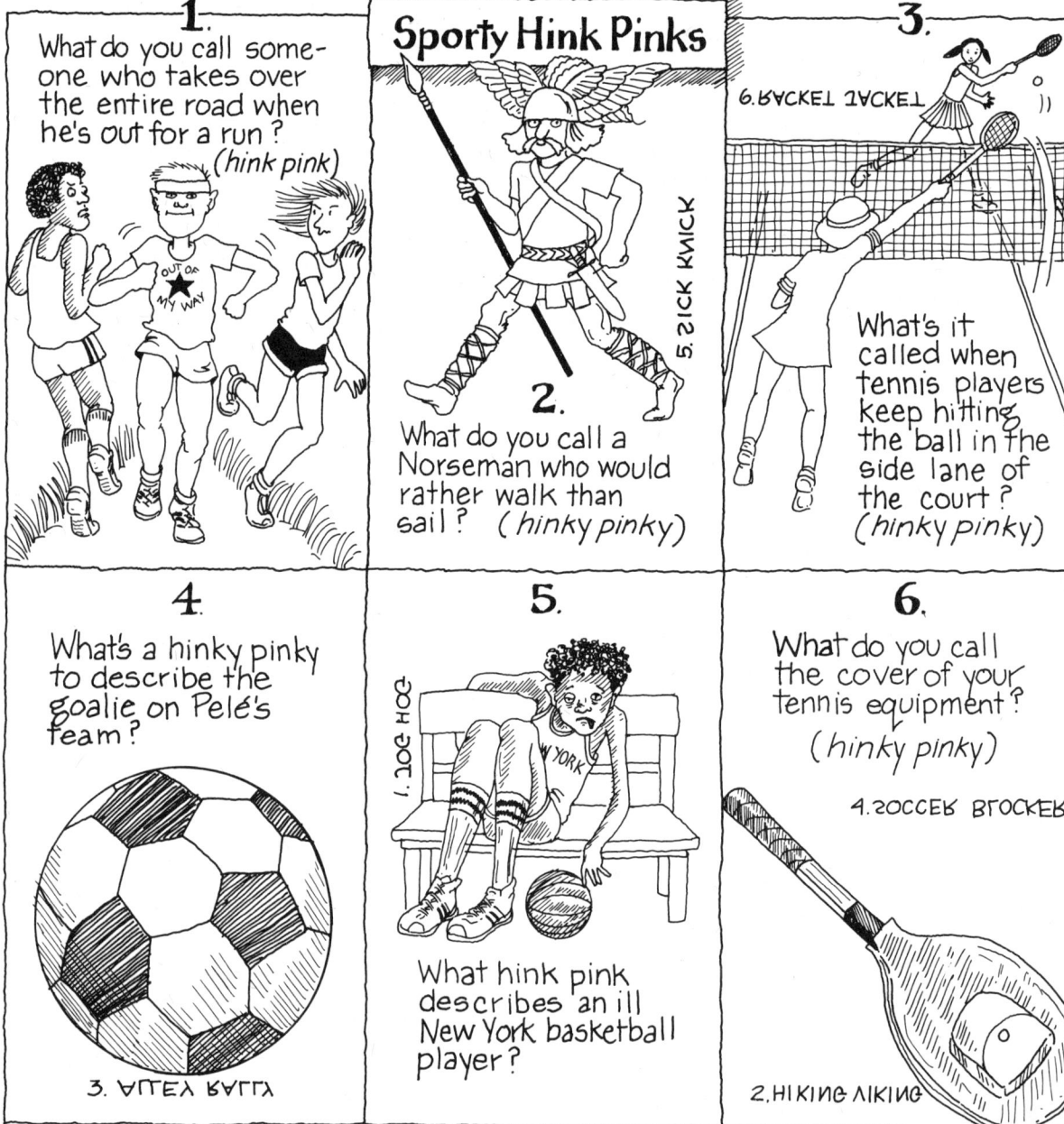

Invitation to a Halloween Hink Pink Dinner

Would you like to come to a special Halloween dinner? Just walk down (__1__) to the house with the (__2__) outside. You'll know when you've found the right place — just listen for the (__3__). Come in, if you dare, to the room with the (__4__) and the (__5__) slouched at the table. Join this (__6__) at the table. Don't be nervous. *Heh, heh.* Have a glass of (__7__) and listen to the (__8__) old jelly bones is telling while you wait for the food to be served. Don't wonder about the other guests. Just relax. *Hee, hee.* And enjoy this (__9__), if you can.

10. GHOST TOAST
11. SNAKE CAKE
12. NOODLES POODLES
13. CHILLING FILLING
14. GUTTER BUTTER
15. WIZARDS' GIZZARDS
16. MUSTARD CUSTARD
17. CRUDE FOOD
18. DINNER DINNER

You'll be feasting on (__10__) stuffed with a (__11__) of (__12__). On the side will be served (__13__), topped with plenty of (__14__). And for dessert? We bet you can hardly wait for this treat of (__15__) with (__16__) on top. Some people think this is absolutely (__17__). But not us. We know it's a (__18__), perfect fare for a good scare. *Heh, heh, heh!*

Clues for the Halloween Hink Pink Dinner

1. A street named after a froglike creature (*hink pink*)
2. A horrifying, revolting pair (*hinky pinky*)
3. The moan of a wise bird (*hink pink*)
4. The top part of a room with its surface coming off (*hinky pinky*)
5. A bony structure made from a Jell-o-like substance (*hinkety pinkety*)
6. A fake framework of a body (*hinky pinky*)
7. A drink made from eight-legged animals (*hinky pinky*)
8. A bloody tale (*hinky pinky*)
9. An imaginary, fantastic supper (*hink pink*)
10. Oven-baked spirit (*hink pink*)
11. An inside that produces cold fear (*hinky pinky*)
12. Internal organs of sorcerers (*hinky pinky*)
13. Macaroni made from French dogs (*hinky pinky*)
14. A substance made from churning milk that was kept in a dirty street (*hinky pinky*)
15. Pastry made from a reptile (*hink pink*)
16. Pudding made from the yellow topping usually used on hot dogs. (*hinky pinky*)
17. Vulgar eatables (*hink pink*)
18. A first-prize meal (*hinky pinky*)

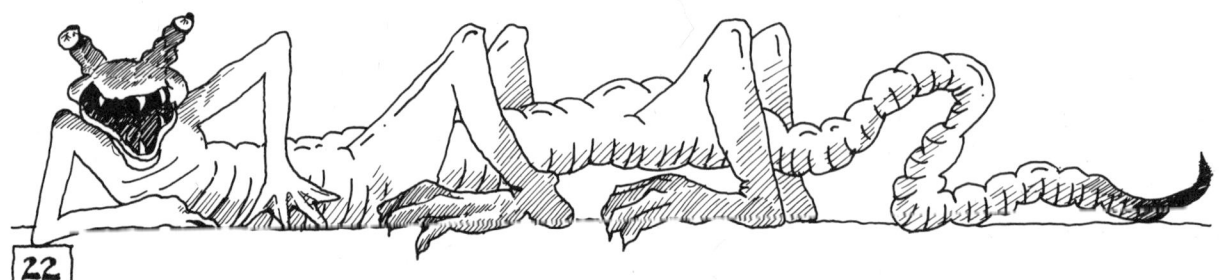

5.
What's a hink pink for a ball hit way up into the air to the center fielder?

1. HEFTY LEFTY

The longest professional baseball game on record went 33 innings. It lasted eight hours and twenty-six minutes. It took place in 1981; The Pawtucket Red Sox beat the Rochester Red Wings, 3 to 2.

2. SPITTER HITTER

3. BUBBLE TROUBLE

6.
What do you call a New York baseball player who's in a bad mood?

(hinky pinky)

4. RECEIVER RELIEVER

Ty Cobb stole home 35 times in his lifetime. That record hasn't been matched yet.

Stan Musial of the St. Louis Cardinals hit five home runs in one day, during a double header against the New York Giants, on May 2, 1954.

25

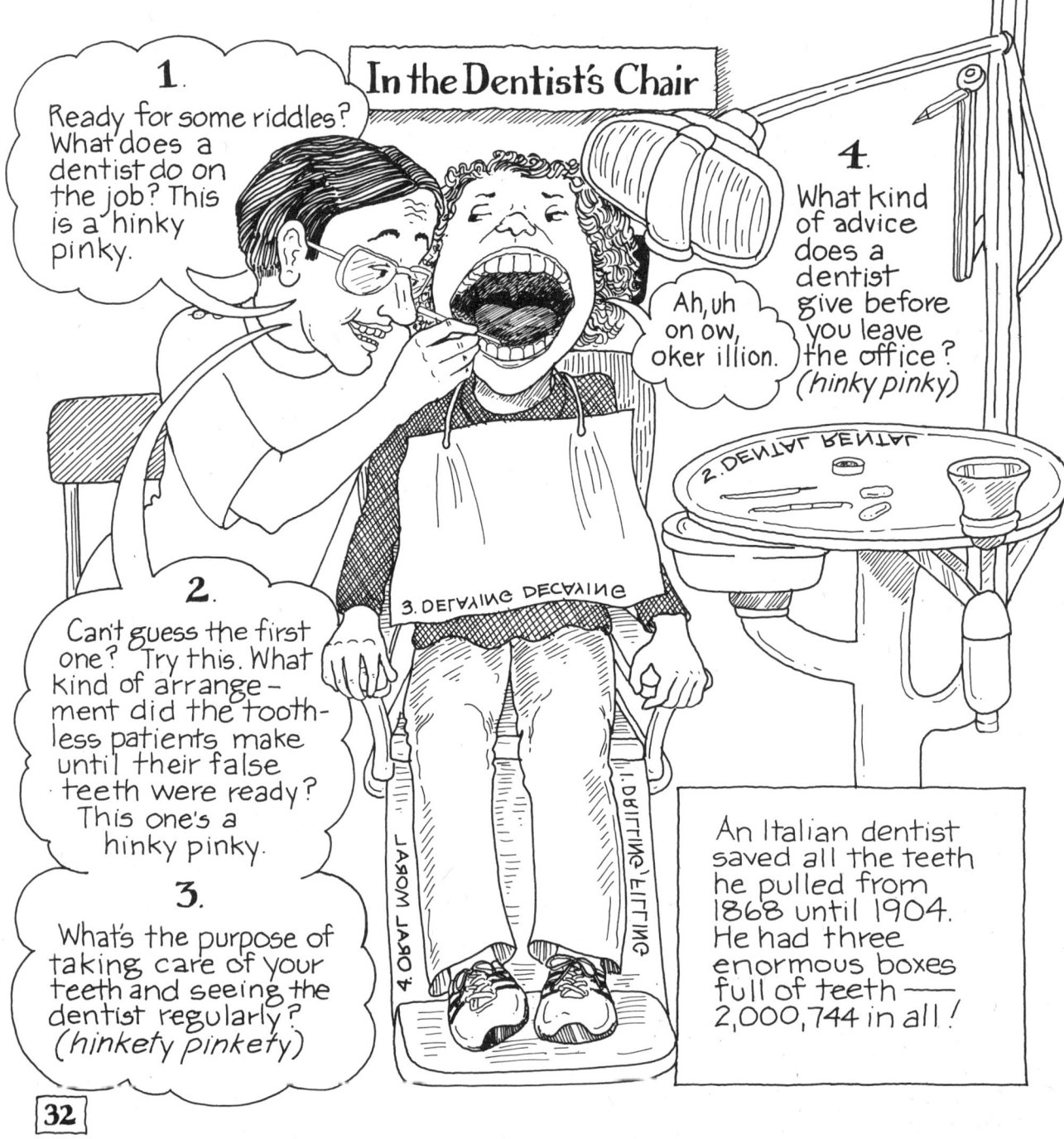

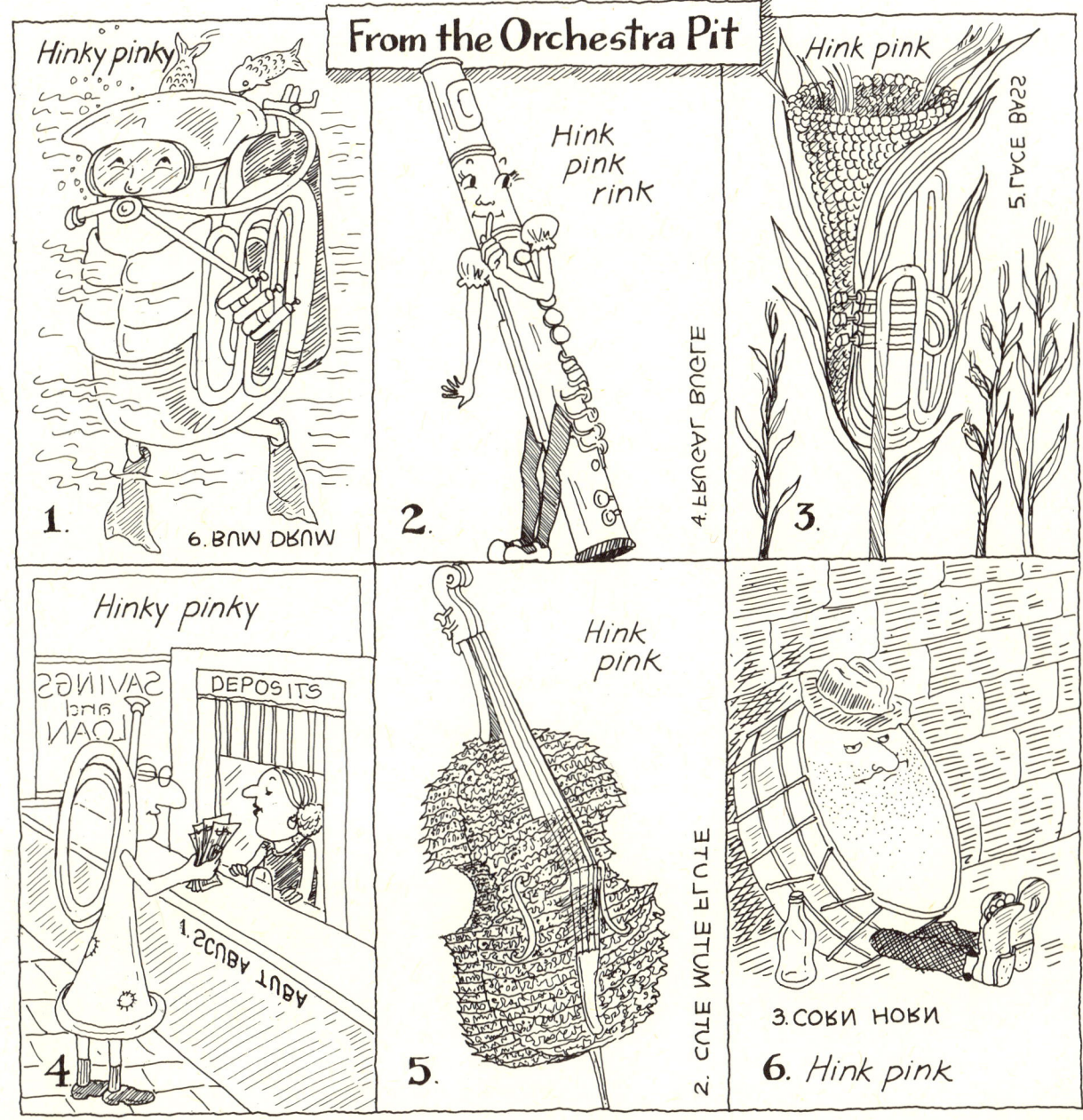

Riddles about Rabbits

1. What did the baby rabbit get for allowance? *(hinky pinky)*

2. What is a comical rabbit? This is a hinky pinky.

The **largest litter** ever known to be born to a pet rabbit was a litter of 24 babies born to a New Zealand white.

3. Thumping, nose twitching and eating carrots are all examples of these. *(hinky pinky)*

It's been reported that the best way to catch a rabbit is to stand behind a tree and make a noise like a carrot. What do you think?

1. BUNNY MONEY
2. FUNNY BUNNY
3. RABBIT'S HABITS

A Hink Pink Mystery

Here is the comical chronicle of the notorious shoe thief, the dreaded (__1__)! For years, this creature stole people's shoes right off their feet, without getting caught, causing a real (__2__). It seemed this robber would never be captured. When it came to tracking this criminal, people just got cold feet.

How did the thief pull off the (__3__)? And (__4__) were stolen? Well, all kinds of shoes were taken, but a favorite target was ballerinas' dance shoes. In the middle of a (__5__), when a ballerina would leap up into the air, a hand would reach up from behind some prop and snatch her shoes right off her feet! The (__6__) would then sneak silently away and disappear, without leaving a single (__7__), while back on stage, (__8__).

Finally the star ballerina hired a (__9__) to capture the vandal.

The spy disguised herself as the star's driver, wearing a snappy uniform and shiny new shoes. The night of the next ballet performance, she waited outside by the car, pretending to read. She made sure that both (__10__) were in clear view. Suddenly she felt a tug at her foot. One (__11__) was off and the thief was grabbing the other! Our heroine jumped on the vandal and there was a (__12__) before the thief was under control. The spy then radioed the nearby police with her (__13__).

"Oooh, ahhh," cried the thief when the police arrived, "I (__14__)."

"Why, you clever (__15__)," said the police, looking down. "No wonder you creep so quietly. You're only wearing tights." And they all stared at the (__16__).

The ballerinas were filled with (__17__) and danced all night for joy. The spy was paid a (__18__), but nobody ever found all the stolen shoes.

·—•—·

Clues for the Hink Pink Mystery

1. A thief who steals summer shoes *(hinky pinky)*
2. A shocking experience about summer shoes *(hinky pinky)*
3. Thefts of shoes without straps or laces *(hinky pinky)*
4. The question asked to determine ownership of footwear *(hink pink)*
5. A performance of ballerinas *(hink pink)*
6. Another name for the ballet shoe thief *(hinky pinky)*
7. Evidence of the stolen footwear *(hink pink)*
8. How the girl described her feet after she'd lost her shoes on a very cold day *(hink pink rink)*
9. A sneaky sleuth *(hink pink)*
10. Shoes that someone hired to drive someone else's car might wear *(hinky pinky)*
11. A foot covering the color of the sky on a clear day *(hink pink)*
12. A little scuffle *(hink pink)*
13. A device to communicate with someone else who isn't within hearing distance *(hinky pinky)*
14. To hate being taken in by a policeman *(hinky pinky)*
15. A greedy wooden-shoe person *(hink pink)*
16. A startling foot covering usually worn under shoes *(hinky pinky)*
17. Wonderful pleasure about someone being caught *(hinky pinky)*
18. A generous fee as a reward *(hinky pinky)*

Answers

1. SANDAL VANDAL
2. SANDAL SCANDAL
3. SLIPPERS' RIPOFFS
4. WHOSE SHOES
5. TOE SHOW
6. SLIPPER CLIPPER
7. SHOE CLUE
8. THOSE TOES FROZE
9. SLY SPY
10. CHAUFFEURS' LOAFERS
11. BLUE SHOE
12. SMALL BRAWL
13. WALKIE TALKIE
14. DETEST ARREST
15. CLOG HOG
16. SHOCKING STOCKINGS
17. CAPTURE RAPTURE
18. HANDSOME RANSOM

HERITAGE INTERMEDIATE SCHOOL
MEDIA CENTER